The Book Of Whimsies

Copyright

© C S Hughes

All rights reserved.

Published in the Commonwealth

ISBN 978-0-9945175-6-2

Second Printing, December, 2018

Published by
Maximum Felix Media
PO Box 440
Korumburra VIC 3950
Australia

For Billy, who was lost,

and the one who found him.

Contents

Spectroscopy

Dragonfly Days

Country Town

Billy Ruffian Hitchhikes Across The Country And Anthropomorphises The Sky

Canute

Chicken Little

Love Poem Number Three

A Dance For Fools

Big The Sky

Billy Ruffian's Manifesto

Fall

Save Saturday A Welkin Watch

Gravity's Misrule

Shall Not The Moon

In Blue Careen

A Prisoner Of This Tower

Ghost

Billy Ruffian On A Pin

Shall We Go To Dunsany?

Sometimes The Moon

Another Poem Tells Billy Ruffian What To Do

Agony Of A Lost Teenage Disco

Peppertrees

Cardboard Titanic

Glister

Dapple

Fossil

Poor Mr Scare

Below The Moon

Every Road Takes You Down

This Day Has Hooks

A Sailor's Lament

An Angel Drums The Boards

In The Park With Billy Ruffian

Absinthe

Aeroplane

Blueshift

Church Street Reminiscence

Big Business

Sirtaki

Old

A Spell Under The Moon To Call A Kiss From A Lost Love's Ghost So As To Know Of The Future

Pinwheels For Their Majesties' Delight

Lunatic

Tea With The Moon

The Last Days Of Billy Ruffian

A Wizard Of The Sundered World

Rainy Tuesday

A Recipe For Christmas Pudding

Christmas Box

Kitchen

A Poem For You And The End Of Time

Weary Stone

Rain Prayer

Venice

Lafferty 's Funeral

Waiting Room

Blue Winter Day

Bluster

Spectroscopy

I shall gather stars in this book

Pressed like fallen leaves

In all their splendoured indifference

So that when at last you fly amongst them

Kicking up storms and weeping over the traces

You will know radiance

Dragonfly Days

Lazarus day is a day for fishing

Forsaking hand and hook and net and bait

A line cast deep

To catch in sudden ripples on slow water

The bare and crystal hum of dragonfly days

Darting past

On thick air the tremolo of unremembered fevers

A chorus in the skin of broken mud

Resounding cautious silences

With wet and aching fingers

A boat of woven grass

To carry away the treasure from the sun

Country Town

Burn these flowers

They sting like hay and tar

The road a mirage in this shimmer day

Where you threw them down

Pulls at your soles - you will never leave

This angry town of brick and tin

The only thing that holds you

Is the rail on your back

And another lorn and dusty voice

On someone else's radio

Billy Ruffian Hitchhikes Across The Country

Leaves in your hair

Ratatat shoes

Dirty black soles

Nothing to lose

Left a girl with a blue song

For a ramshackle day

Bore a broken old cross

For a wing and a prayer

Found in the desert

Lost in the sea

The big empty sky

Looking at me

Canute

Mary and me

Go to the sea

Collecting shells

And anemones

A symmetry

Of castles grow

On my hands

And on my toes

Until with sunset's kingdom falling

In the turn of uncommon tide

I stand

Bucket and spade

Time hewn glass

Lost like footprints

Driftwood man

Only you, only me

Salt between

Clasping hands

Who will say

Bowed to the sun

We once walked here?

Chicken Little

Lost my hat

Lost my words

Before the wind

They've fled like birds

You have tatter wings

Weak from flying

To bright these blue corridors

Bring your black looks

Bring your groans

I will take you dancing

Til you throw away your shoes

I am taken in

By your wayward arms

You have held a shape like easy days

With glad hands

To warn the sky from falling

I am fooled again

Love Poem Number Three

How is this a love poem?

How is it not?

It doesn't wax

It doesn't wane

It doesn't even quite refrain

It just asks this;

What better end but to die

Foolishly hoping

To embrace the Moon?

A Dance For Fools

I have caught the wind in woven reeds

I have made this basket set with coloured stones

You shall embark with kings and butter biscuits

You are a submarine

I have gathered ashes for your casket

Bright with weeds to forsake jewels

We have danced upon a falling shore

We have lost our feathered hats like fools

The Moon has bathed my fallen face in silver

In the sighing of her days I carry you

Big The Sky

I think about how big the sky

I think about how bright the leaf

I think about how you cannot hold

The one without the other

I think about how deep the earth

I think about how cold the sea

That tousling in this wayward skin

Makes these days of fire

I think about how small your hand

I think about how strange your smile

That with a finger to your lips

Encompasses all of me

Billy Ruffian's Manifesto

A hat for the sky to keep me unburnt

A poem in my head to keep me unlearnt

A coin for your love to keep me unearnt

A dream out of hand to keep me unearthed

A hole through the day and an ache through the night

A spoon full of sunshine brutal and bright

Fall

If I could break the sky

To let the stars fall in

Perhaps then I could fly

In that inkling flood

And all the many morning bright and winter cruel

Stalking as they sing

Could admire as they in rapture tear

At these sleight and tumble tatter wings

Save Saturday A Welkin Watch

These shadows stripe your face

Thrown in moonsavage night

Unhinge the barbarous door

Throw it down to heed the mark

Of vicious parallelogram

Cast up your savager eyes

Save Saturday a welkin watch

To bless abandoned sky

In your silence, rust

Fly back these retrograde angels

Their swords that arc in callous disarray

Just tears to welt the skin

Of your once and wheeling wept

Saturnine day eye

Gravity's Misrule

This dismembered thought

On its lack worn wings

Bore me short of breath

Above the wearied stones

Dizzy below the ether

To this railing precipice

A bridge between now here now there

Where we stand upon the edge

To weigh this savager fear

That by misrule you will jump

Or by mischance will fall

While I unlace my leaden boots and in wonder wait

For all this great and cruel geometry to tumble down

The Moon come sailing by

And leave me falling upwards

Stranded in the sky

Shall Not The Moon

You shall not go up to the Moon

You shall not go there now or soon

You shall not see her milky cow

You shall not go there then or now

You shall not see the big earth rise

You shall not see her strange dark side

You shall not sail her dusty seas

You shall not taste her fine green cheese

Hand in hand we shall wait

Dancing in her pale smile

Until night's majesty brooks no delay

And falls to earth to stay awhile

In Blue Careen

Close your eyes stop your mouth you cannot see me

My fierce sun you come and go in radiance

Leaven blind these sundog ghosts haunting heaven

Winged cerulean

Flown away to own one ache, the sky destroys

Roar these wings tied up in bows, nor sing nor fly

Defy desire to ascend, this hungered fall

Quiet air

Let go reason

Find the wood beneath

Stand beside the sun

So you don't blind me

When I stagger let me fall

So I may hide in shadow at your feet

It is your bent arm that compels to flight

The tendons in your neck

To tie in knots these flowers for a bridle

These for a crown

Where you lead upon my want

So I may follow

A Prisoner Of This Tower

Wear your black cloth and your silver

He who commands the sword

Bears the weight

As much as the hand

Of whom is weldt

Raise black wings

The crows have took my eyes

In their talons murder high

So I in my red blind dark

May espy the derang'd ground

That sates the raven of his carnage

The place for peace is a hollowed place

The iron frets the crown that rings this caul

The emptiness makes the cage

As the scaffold makes the wall

Ghost

I think I will complain

How the Moon made you look

A shroud of frost in still dark day

That when I reach with careful hand to touch

Fall to dust

It was this that made me say I want to steal

When all I want is to imagine your cold breath

In the blush of dawn against my lips

To hold in silence this unquiet and unpromised kiss

Billy Ruffian On A Pin

She is small

She knows the things she holds divine

The way that dancing with this chair leaves a scar

Hold her, let her go

She knows not tears

But dervish 'round and falling

Will change the courses of the stars

The way she recites in ecstasy

And I cajole in shame

Under moonlight

Is no less than the game

And no more

Than the confusion of a kiss

On another lost and doldrum evening

Shall We Go To Dunsany?

Rain child with your wooden things

Gripped tight in pale fingers

Sleep has left you bruised around the eyes

Admiring from the windowsill

Where the paint is cracked like skin

The willows atremble bowing in the storm

Shaking droplets like a veil

Railing at the fixity of their roots

Oh to go

Marching not to Dunsinane

But to green and hallowed hills

Forgo the meat and the bread

Take only a little honey to forget

Hollow out your bones

So you may fly and follow them

Sometimes The Moon

I shall purloin these words like a charlatan

Sounding rough songs so the Moon may hear

Oh so dog-faced and weary-wise

The Moon tomorrow upholds the heavens

So you may lie late dreaming

You who mix in equal measure artifice and scorn

Scoffing with studied guile disdain the Moon

Here below your strident truths we bask and dance

The Moon and I scoff in turns at you

Another Poem Tells Billy Ruffian What To Do

Kick this sleeping dog

Let it lie

Fetch a glass for me

And for your ghost

Give me your honest eyes

And a few coins to get to heaven

Steal my silver spoon

That I stole

Light these lesser fires

Hold your breath

Let go this rope

Count to seven

Agony Of A Lost Teenage Disco

I am a cornice forgetting myself

I am the vines that etch in regret red brick walls

Listening for the solemn silence

That promises all things fall

I have fled from songs

Coughing blue smoke

Athwart this giant's causeway

Of tumble down TVs

fool, how you implored

In desperation's disco

Finding in uncouth gyrations grinning escape

While you savage wallflower agonies

I scuff the earth to mark contrary blessings

And won my crown of grass in nowhere town

Peppertrees

Will you give me days of quiet ruin

In these chains of care

If you see me standing where the iron

In corrugations dogs the sun

To hide forlorn and bone-bare dreams

Where lizards tongue the rust red stains

Hoping to taste blood

I will take from you the cloy-sweet trees

Where in that ragged cloth you were bound

Where cutting short your delinquent hair

Freed but did not save us

From the glorious injuries

Of our careening innocence

Cardboard Titanic

You shall fall in love with dead people and with cats

I will float above the clouds

Lowering hooks to startle birds

And torment from them screeching reason

Adrift on a salt laden sea

Where uttered ecstasies roll and tumble

Swelling like a state of grace

To fall in storms and dash in wreckage

Upon proud promenades

Frightened leviathans will wrap in loving grasp

Lumbering behemoths

Down down down

We shall crash dinghies to sink icebergs

And doff our caps to citizens of marooned civilizations

That from the shore of sinking islands

In desperation wave

Begging for a word

Glister

There is a city in the sky

Where spires bright make arcs of gold

And all the lordly passing by

Take a fright, below

There is a machine inside your eye

That makes the sun in its travail

And all the planets in raiment beam

These fierce trajectories to circumscribe

An ideocentric universe, where

In her shining mystery

From that tower she declines

To offer solace

Only pledging with sad smile

All that strangely glisters

Dapple

I will walk with you

short of breath, to the shore

Where the sunshine makes a beast

Of your arms

Saying, not goodbye, but a river

Where it bends

Beneath these hills and trees

This surface dapple blinding

As close I come to your wake

These pent waves disintegrate

Fossil

I will love you with my sleeves rolled up

I will love you with both hands

I will love you with the curving of this back

I will lay the sun upon the ground

The sun is in this spine and in these knuckle bones

With a fist, a jackboot heat

Still I crook this weight of words to tell

Of how I let the sunshine in

The way I hear the sea inside this shell

Is the way I see the sky upon this bone-bare wing

The way I hold your life from this abandoned cloth

Is the way I hear the prayer

In the hollow of this skull

These abandon eyes hold still the turning days

While I love you with the ache

In the hollow of these arms

This fossil spine

These bones a mountain

Poor Mr Scare

I am here to scare

The crows my dear

Though they are mostly laughing

With disdain

As they peck and tear

At my poor stuffing

And harry me

In their desultory way

Am I perturbed

Or are they?

Disturbed and mystified

Expecting tasty guts

And finding rotten hay

Go goresome bird!

No rubies red

For you today

Below The Moon

On silent wing

Where ravens claw

Where caged birds sing

A king of owls

Lost his crown

Hanging from the hookéd Moon

Where the lord of night makes silver

I flew too high

I flew too soon

I flew too close to the hookéd Moon

Whither it fell by field or sea

Or where the lord of night does frown

I do not know

The parliament of owls decree

Whomsoever find it

Our liege lord shall be

Grim in black and midnight mayhem

Oh be not proud

Cried the raven

Redly eyed

Who spied them

I have no taste for a crown

Unless it be a ring of bones

Half buried in the earth

Richly jewelled in sinew and in flesh

With the sun from my black wings to warm it

But I saw the shining thing where it fallen

Where your moondrunk master let it be

A horn to call the morning and the night

Silent as the nightbird's wing is silver

In the roil toil mist and mael sea

Come my lords

Set me free from your cruel hooks

Come thee by dear Pluto's shore and look!

O black-tongued bird prone in defeat

Leave off your grim and midnight mayhem

Tell me why I should not make of you my meat?

My Lord, while I am not a feast

Suitable for bird nor beast

You have lost your clumsy crown

And if your lordships set me down and fly

I will show you where to find it

For it is law amongst the parliament of owls

That some wear wise and some wear cowls

For want of a crown all is lost

Follow by me

And where the owl lords bent by the shore

Around his night and tatter skull

In the red and roil sea

The hornéd crown adorned him

All the owls in their frowns bowed low

And that is why

Above the sea

Below the Moon

In haunt and hallow trees

A rag and tatter raven

Rules the sky

King of owls and feasts

Every Road Takes You Down

Clouds fall apart

Like dead flamingos

Adrift in acid skies

A violence too bruised for evening's stars

I have no use for you

I hear the needling of this box

The engine that you turn

To revolt this tune

In another tin-eared frenzy

This road takes you down

Trailing forgotten flags

Through the bruise and tatter assault

Of a fool's sun dance

Closing eyes

Untrod in fell inclines

On every road you frayed

Another liar's sunset

Lewd as coal and painted eyes

This Day Has Hooks

Mornings like gravel and glass

I am transparent

Stillness passes through me

Brittle as clocks

Time a bothersome complaint

Screwing their faces

In measures of startle and disdain

The bright reflections

From oddly passing cars

Blanched and deathly screeches

Trammelling flaws

This break and stutter moment hunts like owls

A Sailor's Lament

Galleon ladies in death masks go

Dreaming of lost Mexico

The dead have gathered on the strand

To listen to the echoing

The sea is rising and the sand

Encroach upon this widow's peak

Soldiers red and soldiers blue

Abjure this slow pestilence

The brigantessas to and fro

Worry oar locks where follow

By my cull and clinker boat

Sailfish on the wing

Clean the ashes from your hands

Taste this salt to reminisce

An Angel Drums The Boards

A sad and savage day

A day for ink to mark

In thoughtless stripes

This howl's tongue

A day to poison widow's weeds

In ferrous and in nitre

A stain like blood leaves dead man's shoes

In a wire jig

Knots at elbow, neck and wing

To laugh a spiter's nose

In ferocious evensong

From this clown and hallow face

In The Park With Billy Ruffian

I can hear antarctica falling in the sea

My ear against the opera that echoes in this shell

You say diamonds are the hardest thing of all

I offer this cold concrete when you fall

For a while, away from where this world abrades

And makes of all this shining glass

Prosceniums of need and loss

Actors all unwitting

A papillon tangled in your hair

Does not mean you're free

And for these monday morning thoughts a fever

Billy Ruffian slept in the park

Woke with upside bats and downside larks

And watched the inkness wander in their skins

Not knowing which way out

Where the concrete shone with cold

And the hard crept in

All the stars lost in the dark

Broken window glass

Stale bread and tea

All tattoos go to heaven

To leave the skin quite clean

Absinthe

Shall we gather at the mountain of martyrs

Where this mourning trumpet rues the day

You and I to lose our somnolent consequences

In the smoke of strange tobaccos and burnt chartreuse

You will tell me —this is not a dream

But a colour like a bruise

While a sunbright angel mourns the night

And we admire with silk-wet smiles

Those in summer dresses and winter shoes

That saunter by in negligence and feign

Our sad and laughing admiration to disdain

Aeroplane

I shall follow these gravel lines

Raising wayward dust dry upon the tongue

Like saltbush and spinifex

On this high and mighty bluff

I shall find a gravelling place to be alone

Can you not hear

Like some dreaming God

You have twice as many ears as faces

To hold up high your head

I shall toss my hat

At the millinery industrial complex

And watch it come tumbling down

Ribands trailing

I have taken your picture

Not to cherish but to erase you

I will kill you three times

Once with loss

Once with this maudlin tree

Once with the articles of war

Once in red-faced glee

What is this threat in mathematics

That you will count until I obey

A dance above the grave lines

With this airplane I thin the sky

Leaving curls of clouds and blue

The pressure that lifts you up

Low above your wing and high below

Blueshift

Spindle limb and candle face

To cool the knots of sweat that bring this fever

I will hang my head in joy

From the window of another fast moving train

These pylons in acerbic cyphers

Oscillate like sirens

Singing gravel

Wire hum

Another monotonous song

Until in dogged day an oncoming train

Where my doppelgänger shouts

Dares me to shut my mouth

Church Street Reminiscence

Bring me the sugar and the tea

Sweet and bitter like a mourning song

A nice record for a funeral

From dust ye came, dust ye will be

Let me blow kisses to the dead girls

Looking back with marble eyes

Here now I have a slim advantage

In that I can still love them

But they cannot love me back

I will raise my styrene cup and bow

We will boast with shameful politics

Talking of battles we never fought

And sunken ships and angels

And cities underground

But not the poison or the ichorous lament

Weeping from sepia portraits

The winsome smile on cyanide lips

That brought them here

Big Business

If I had a responsible job

I would wear my pyjamas to work

They have little fishes on and worn out hems

So attired I would command

Sifting the dire consequences of fiscal probity

And managerial ruin

Through the shapes of dragons and lambs

Clouds drifting against

The unambiguous blue of towering facades

I would fill the water cooler with lime punch

And ambush cubicants to discuss which would be longer

If the world were bisected equatorwise

The length of a yoyo string

Or the surface the spiral groove of a record

And spinning what music would it play?

Given the key to the executive bathroom

I would block the drains with pencil erasers

And turn on all the taps

To see if filled clear and blue

With ink stained water

Pens and cables and laptops

Secretaries and chairs and sheafs of copy paper

Floating through corridors and colliding in boardrooms

Whether this aquarium would entertain

For more than a season

Of peculiar faces glub glubbing at the glass

Or all the bright and razor fish

Would die of *cause célèbres* and neglect

Drawing the plug and flushing the sad denizens

Into a culvert to the tempered and forgetting sea

Sirtaki

I see you curling and swooping

Poised on a fulcrum

A lever long enough to unbalance the world

I will dance with you when you are dead

Here you are gathered

In this sheet of light

Swaying and calling

To where in this radiance

I shine and weep

Here are the dead words

Dry on the tongue

Each echo lost with the dust

Of cities sunken

Ah, for my thirst give me wine

And on this rubble we will dance

And again forget the words

Of this forgotten song

Old

Now I am old I will be a poet

Stumble-tongued in slipshod shoes

My pockets filled with ramshackle words

My wonderings worn at heel

My heart cloud-thin

Bearing the weight of coloured stones

Gathered in sun and sorrow

Scattered along the silver road

My feet now find bare purchase

Tousling the tops of trees

Unwrought above the falling hills

By those same yearnings

This neglectful child ever had to fill a song

A Spell Under The Moon

Oh in brigand argent

Falling down the sky

This storm a shroud in tatter-glow

Bow to join the dance

From this bier of treasure and tricks

Where I hide your waxen mask

With this ribbon unshrive your locks

I will knot old lumpen face

In this broken cup

And taste the gravedew on your lips

To hold the black and rising seas

Of these sweet and argent auguries

Pinwheels For Their Majesties' Delight

The King of Owls doffed his crown

To the Parliament of Crows

The King of Cats summoned rats

And of their guts for bird-black heads made tricorn hats

The Queen of Snows

With her woes

Dealt the dogs a thousand blows

Setting some to whine and some to howling

The Lord of Flies

With his jewelled eyes

Stolen from a million dead

Spoke of angels and of pins

Most eloquently lying

All the blind bent their knees

And from pursed lips paid ghost coins

For the lard in lamplights burning

In the dark from their bowed heads

The crows have torn the eyes

And cast them on the shore

For their Majesties' delight

Where bright a thousand pinwheels

Turning for the dead

Laughing in the storm risen from their wings

Lunatic

I got so drunk

the moon fell down

And broke my head

Now I'm dead but walking 'round

My feet above the boneyard ground

Dancing frost upon the stones

Drink with me her silver wine

And you will know my moonstruck song

Bury me in her yellow light in August

Until that day

We will sing of doom'd voyages and sad kings

And ask of all who come there past

This last mourned mystery

Is the silver in the wine or in the song?

Tea With The Moon

4 am a cup of tea

There is just the Moon and me

And your slow breathing

All the world awaits the march absurd

In homage, as she wanes

You and I (and maybe thee)

In moonmad sorrow to her leaving

Await another word

The Last Days Of Billy Ruffian

Here the sun bastard bright

That once in fevered splendour crowned

Lays a hand upon my brow

Burns my skin

Shuts my eyes

Where tranced in fortune's miseries

The sour old lord

Bloat and red as a dead man's eye

Groans in unheard fury

The road that rolled me six and nine

Leaves me tumbledown

They put me in this box to kill the sky

Now in raven kindness

Us and them

The living and the dead

I have papers I attend

This semi-professional ghost association

No longer walls to deify

These nights shall not regale in stars

But flickering incendiaries

A Wizard Of The Sundered World

I asked the wizard, what's the time?

He said come back at five past nine

And bring me cheeseburgers and beer

Will you hold the tears that sting my eyes?

Stop your machine, stop your wail

There's a hole in the sky that makes you blind

To see it find that between

Where peace still grows in silence

Wizard what is it that broke the world apiece?

Those who when they see a mouse

Instead of sharing this sweet morsel, kill

Have made this sundered world

So they may feast on cochineal and marchpane

If only I could find

Where the mountain makes the sea

They would drown

I could dig with my black thumbs and tatter fingers

To turn the ocean upside down

All the fishwives singing as they marched

Up above

In fearsome breath

All the monsters clawing at the ground

It's six past nine

Rainy Tuesday

Hope is an umbrella that I forgot

Some years ago, in a cafe or on a bus

That wandering out into the storm

Gives me joy that I once and now disdain

Shelter from the recollected rain

A Recipe For Christmas Pudding

Find a hat size six and three

Brim with flour, milk and cream

That you diced for in a dream

With a sea-wracked sailor

Find three lords, wise and true

Give them caps and give them shoes

Give them bibs and give them spoons

And set them then to mixing

Add twelve eggs, roll them 'round

From St Paul's to Camden Town

Check on each that doth not frown

In its roilly rather

Add thee plums for larks and luck

Throw in thruppence from a beggar's cup

Check which face is facing up

To steal the devil's favour

Put the lords to their machine

To make of it a mayhem

Stir until the dough turns gold

Like a king sad lost of old

Gone by sea and maelstrom

Wear it in the noonday sun

Downside up and upside down

From Michaelmas to Hallow's Eve

And whist the Moon has yet begun

Bury deep with these bones

Where the devil dances

On Christmastide dig it up

With custard from your dead dog's eye

Garnish holly poison barb

Feed it to each sweet smiling child

To make a song-sweet praise

Christmas Box

There is silver in this box

And all the things we said

Kindness, tinsel, piercing bright

In convex play our bauble reveries

Derelict soldiers laid with care

Now attention, now at ease

In faded headlines and obituaries

A star that glisters more than gold

A thrice folded tree

Peace, joy, merrily, my love

For the sun in tinsel winter

Packed in this box

Kitchen

This glass is filled with light

That curves the room into a ball

and it fills it with a mercury

That holds all those small convexities we share

The chipped enamel kettle

Black iron showing through the daisies

Is quiet

Drink it down

I'm not sure

When you're not here

If this room is half empty

Or half full

A Poem For You And The End Of Time

If I could make a word

To keep the sunshine in

It would sound just like your name

Only laughing

If I could make a rhyme

To keep the darkness out

It would echo 'round these hills

Until the end of time

If I could make a poem

That freed your heart of doubt

It would whisper from my lips

Until the sun went out

If I could sing a song

To make the Moon our friend

I would ask you of your heart

Not to keep, just to lend

Weary Stone

Shoulders wreck

I am a mountain

A cage of bones

I am what sleeps

Where the snow is thick

Where no ungentle footfalls mark

I take beleaguered steps

To slip on frail ground

Falling avalanche

In quietude that gathers

Where giants quake

To throw off earthbound feet

Rain Prayer

Wear these wings

Say this prayer

If I flight

If I hide

The banished Moon

Will be my light

An airborne beast

Writhe of fang and skein of scale

With clothen hooves

Softly breaks the cloud

These molecules that thunder

Haul the drifting dark

Hear the swathe in tentative march

Alight upon the shingle

Whisper mouthy dead

Crouching creature

Hunt for war

Rattle on this rail

Turning topsy weathervane

Where these wings?

Stay this prayer

Venice

In a city dwelt by whores

It never snows

All the pretty vampires go

Hand in hand through corridors

Of echoing hotels

On the plaza relentless rain

Envelopes the wail bowing waves

Of a shrill departing train

My love I love in winter by the sea

Not brightly coloured things

But blood and seawrack on the sand

Where condemned in cages howl like wolves

You have run from me

Fled a burning building

In your casual arson

I collapse again

My embers rise in admonition

To the bright eternal skies

Above the swell and undivided waves

Lafferty's Funeral

My funeral suit is full of splits

To ensure with ease it fits

That I get dressed on that bright morn

With such dignity it be worn

To tide me through grim limbo

Despite my tongue all poking out

And my arms akimbo

All gathered there will stand a round

And pour it to the hungry ground

To send me on my way

Waiting Room

Everything is strange

Keep calm

This is just the end of things

Remember the smell of stale bread

Toasting until almost burnt

This is our body

An extemporary sacrament

Subluminary in substantiation

Transient but satisfactory as another sip of tea

Out the window

Above the swamp

There is a blue sky fat with buttered scones

Around your heels

Stagnant water

And the drone of dragonfly wings

Call life extinct

A breath a residue

Your woodsmoke heart

Maybe earthquakes make alarums

The whistles of trains hauling rumbling cattle cars

Warn sharply of collision

Here the benches are hard

There is gentle laughter

As dogs sing

Have some jam and cream

Sweet, isn't it?

Blue Winter Day

Got me a hatful of sunshine

A handful of air

A face full of strawberries

A rickety chair

A shoe full of trouble

A fire of tears

A string that is knotted

Too wicked to bear

The bark from this climbing

The sun that is dancing

Through these fallen leaves

My yellow face

The sound of a tree

The sky for a kingdom

The sea for a dream

For a feast from the gods

These apples and pears

Thoughts of your hand as a care

When I have fallen

And wound myself home

Face all a-wry

And broken my head

Unfinding the sky

There you are waiting

At the foot of the stairs

Bluster

I carry the sky

Where I go

Upon my hat

And down below

Beneath my soles

The clouds pass by

With their cheerful whistling

Gathering up a storm or two

To send in raucous whispering

Me my merry earthbound way

Where in devotion daisies sway

To enfold my humble falling

About the Author

C S Hughes grew up on both sides of the tracks in ochre towns and charcoal cities. When he was young he found his way from desert to sea and back again, before getting lost in reading and study. He has lived in parks and palaces and worse places, has been a spice seller, a bookseller, a hobo and a watchmaker. He has previously published *The Art Of Knitting Needle Ikebana*, had short stories and poetry published in *Takahe, Pakeha, Sagacity, Newtown News, Uneven Floor, The Blue Pepper, Weird Tales, A Guide To Sydney Rivers* and *Five 2 One Magazine*, amongst others.

He sometimes writes on popular culture at nerdalicious.com.au

You can also find him and his work at http://facebook.com/cshoose

He says he is getting older but no more wise.

www.ingramcontent.com/pod-product-compliance
Lightning Source LLC
Chambersburg PA
CBHW060500010526
44118CB00018B/2488